# Read & Resp

FOR
**KS2**

---

**SECTION 1**

# The Iron Man

**SECTION 2**

# Guided reading

**SECTION 3**

# Shared reading

**SECTION 4**

# Plot, character and setting

**SECTION 5**

# Talk about it

**SECTION 6**

# Get writing

**SECTION 7**

# Assessment

# Read & Respond

## FOR KS2

**Author:** Jillian Powell

**Editor:** Victoria Lee

**Assistant Editor:** Rachel Mackinnon

**Series Designer:** Anna Oliwa

**Designer:** Helen Taylor

**Illustrations:** Tom Gauld

Text © 2006 Jillian Powell   © 2006 Scholastic Ltd

Designed using Adobe InDesign

Published by Scholastic Ltd, Villiers House,
Clarendon Avenue, Leamington Spa,
Warwickshire CV32 5PR

www.scholastic.co.uk

Printed by Bell & Bain
4 5 6 7 8 9      9 0 1 2 3 4 5

British Library Cataloguing-in-Publication Data
A catalogue record for this book is available from the British
Library.
ISBN 0-439-94495-3   ISBN 978-0439-94495-3

## Acknowledgements
The publishers gratefully acknowledge permission to reproduce
the following copyright material:
**Faber and Faber** for the use of the image of the front cover and
extracts from *The Iron Man* by Ted Hughes © 1968, Ted Hughes
(1968, Faber and Faber). **Tom Gauld** for the use of illustrations
from *The Iron Man* by Ted Hughes © 2005, Tom Gauld (2005,
Faber and Faber).
Every effort has been made to trace copyright holders for the works
reproduced in this book, and the publishers apologise for any
inadvertent omissions.

# The Iron Man

## About the book

*The Iron Man* has become a classic children's story since Ted Hughes first wrote it as a bedtime tale for his own children in 1968. With its gargantuan characters and fabulous plot, the story has been called 'a modern fairy tale'. It has echoes of legend and fable from 'David and Goliath' to 'Beauty and the Beast', as a small boy takes on might and strength, single-handedly and bravely befriending – and so humanising – an iron giant.

In the nature of fairy tale and fable, the story is related in a matter of fact narrative style, and many questions remain unanswered: where does the Iron Man come from? How does the boy Hogarth come to be carrying a nail and a knife, just when he needs them?

The story begins with a mysterious iron giant toppling over a cliff edge and breaking into pieces. In a surreal sequence, and with a prophetic show of character and resilience, the pieces reassemble themselves and the Iron Man returns.

Photo © Caroline Forbes

He goes on a hungry rampage, devouring farm machinery and fencing, provoking the farmers, whose livelihoods he threatens, into a warlike response. It is the farmer's son, Hogarth, who saves him *and* the farmers, by finding a clever solution for both.

When the people of the world face a greater threat, from the colossal space-bat-angel-dragon, the Iron Man becomes their saviour, and a trial of strength by fire brings the story to a fairy-tale happy ending. Within the simple narrative is a weighty theme: the superiority of dialogue and negotiation over futile conflict and war.

## About the author

Ted Hughes was born in Yorkshire in 1930. He spent much of his childhood fishing for pike and shooting with his elder brother on the Yorkshire Moors and once said, 'My first six years shaped everything'. He was encouraged to write by his English teacher and wrote comical verse to amuse his classmates when he was 11.

After Cambridge University, he did a number of jobs, including rose gardener, night watchman, zoo attendant and school teacher before his first major success with the poems published as *The Hawk in the Rain* in 1957.

In 1961, Hughes moved to Devon, where he lived for the rest of his life, farming, writing, walking on Dartmoor, and driving round in his old Morris car. He married twice. His first wife, the poet Sylvia Plath, died tragically in 1963. He later married again, and his second wife, Carol Orchard, outlived him.

Hughes said he wrote about the things he was most fond of – 'birds, beasts, fish and the rest.' He was awarded an OBE in 1977 and was Poet Laureate from 1984 until his death in 1998.

### Facts and figures
*The Iron Man*
First published in 1968
Over a million copies sold
Featured on television's *Jackanory* in 1986
Adapted into a rock musical composed by Pete Townshend of The Who in 1989
Made into an animated film, *The Iron Giant* (Warner Bros) in 1999
A sequel to the book, *The Iron Woman*, was published in 1993.

# Guided reading

## First reading

The first reading should be used to familiarise the children with the story and introduce the characters and key themes.

## Expectations

Look together at the cover of *The Iron Man*. Ask the children what they think the story is about – what do they learn from the title and illustration? Now turn to the back cover and read the blurb together. Ask what more they have learned about the story – what kind of story is it going to be? What other 'fairy tales' do the children know? What do they think the characteristics of a fairy story are, in terms of character, setting or plot? (For example: heroes and heroines; good and bad characters; a magical or fantastical setting or events; a happy ending.)

## The Iron Man

Read the first chapter with the children. Ask them to summarise the scene described. Where do they think the Iron Man has come from? Can they suggest why he steps over the cliff or goes into the sea at the end of the chapter? Before beginning Chapter 2, ask the children to look at the illustration and consider what might be going to happen next. Read as far as '…there were big teeth-marks in the steel.' Ask the children what they think has happened. What does this tell them about the Iron Man? How do they think the farmers will react?

Read on to: 'They were certain now that they'd get him.' Ask the children to explain what the farmers are planning to do. (Lure him with a bait so he falls into the trap.) Explain that this kind of trap has often been used to trap animals in the wild. What do the children think the farmers will do with the Iron Man if they catch him?

Finish the chapter together and ask the children to explain what has happened. How does Hogarth attract the Iron Man? How does he feel when he has trapped him? Do the children think the Iron Man has feelings and, if so, can they suggest any evidence for it?

Look at the illustration at the start of Chapter 3. Ask the children to describe what it shows, and what they think might be going to happen. Read to the end of the chapter. Why is the Iron Man 'in heaven'? How does Hogarth's plan help him *and* the farmers?

## The space-bat-angel-dragon

Read together Chapter 4. How are the people of the Earth trying to solve the problem of the space-bat-angel-dragon? How is this similar to the way the farmers tried to deal with the Iron Man? Ask the children what Hogarth suggests instead.

Finish the story together and ask the children to summarise what happens in the last chapter. Does the story have a fairy-tale ending, and if so how?

## Second reading

Subsequent readings allow the children to examine the issues in the story in more depth. As they already know the story they can concentrate on how themes and characters are developed.

## Problem and resolution

Re-read the first chapter together. Discuss the idea of an iron giant as a fairy-tale character. Tell the children that, when Ted Hughes was growing up in the 1930s and 1940s, the first metal robots were appearing as toys and in films and adventure serials. Discuss some of the mysteries about the Iron Man – where do the children think he comes from? Why might he have never seen the sea? Do they think he is just mechanical parts – like a robot? What do they imagine he has inside him? When do his eyes change colour and what do the children think that might show?

Look again at the illustration at the beginning of Chapter 2. How would the children describe the mood and feel of the scene? Hogarth is

# Guided reading

fishing, alone. How is he a 'lone' figure in this story? What does he do or say that sets him apart from the farmers and the people of the world?

Read on through Chapter 2, and then recap on some of the key points in the chapter. Ask the children how they feel about the Iron Man when he topples over the cliff, and later when he falls into the trap. Encourage them to support their answers with reasons. Ask the children why they think Hogarth wants to use the hole to catch a fox. Why do they think he is carrying a long nail and a knife in his pocket? (Do they think these things need to be explained to make the story work?) Discuss the idea that in fairy tales and fables, things sometimes happen that are not explained but that move the action along.

Read Chapter 3 together, asking for volunteers to read the parts of the family having the picnic. Pause at the paragraph beginning: 'The farmers came near...' Focus on the similes: 'His chest was as big as a cattle truck. His arms were like cranes...' Can the children recall any of the other similes used to describe the Iron Man? (For example: '...the great iron head, square like a bedroom...') Ask them how these similes help the reader to imagine him. (By comparing him to familiar things.)

Pause at the end of Chapter 3 and ask the children if they think the story could end here. Why? (Hogarth has sorted the problem of the Iron Man, and there is a happy ending.) Ask the children: what is about to happen next? How are the two main episodes linked? Read out the words: 'Hogarth visited the Iron Man every few days.' Ask the children how befriending the Iron Man is going to help Hogarth in the second half of the story.

## Stargazing

Begin reading Chapter 4 and ask the children if they can explain what a constellation is. (A group or formation of stars.) Read as far as '...hitting a bowl of goldfish.' Ask the children to count the number of times the word 'bigger' is used. Read the phrase '...grew and Grew and GREW.' What does the writer use other than

repetition to emphasise certain words on this page? (Progressive use of capital letters.)

Look at the lines: 'Faster than a bullet. Faster than any rocket. Faster even than a meteorite.' Ask the children if they are complete sentences. Why not? (They do not have a subject or verb.) Can they add words to make them complete sentences? Ask the children why they think the writer has written in this way. (It speeds up the pace, to reflect the speed of the star.)

Read as far as the words: '...and it was a terrific dragon.' Ask the children how the writer creates the suspense of waiting. How many different creatures is the thing from space compared to, as the writer builds up the image? (Four.) What do they all share in common? (They all have wings.)

Focus on the onomatopoeic word 'Barrrump'. Ask the children if they think they could find this word in the dictionary. How is the writer using it here? Ask them if they can remember how the writer described the sound of the Iron Man falling down the cliff, and refer back to the opening of the book.

Read on to the end of the chapter, and ask the children what problem faces the people of the world now? How is it similar to the problem the farmers had with the Iron Man and how is it different and worse? What size is the Iron Man in comparison with the space-bat-angel-dragon? They both have huge appetites, but what does each need to be fed with?

## Trial by fire

Continue reading Chapter 5 as far as: '...he could flatten the Iron Man with one eyelash.' Ask the children to summarise the Iron Man's challenge – and explain what the test of strength will be. Why do they think he chooses fire and heat? Explain that metals like iron have a high melting point: they can be heated to high temperatures without melting. What sort of test of strength might the dragon have chosen instead?

Read on to the end of the chapter. Ask the children how many trials the Iron Man and the space-bat-angel-dragon enter into. Ask the children if they have heard the popular expression

# Guided reading

'trial by fire'. Do they know what it means? (A test of someone's abilities under pressure.)

How would they describe the Iron Man's character as he undergoes his ordeal? At the end of the story, what are the battle scars he has to show the trials he has been through in the story? (He has lost one ear, and the other has begun to melt.) How do the children feel towards him, and towards the space-bat-angel-dragon?

Read out the phrase 'the music of the spheres' and ask the children if they have heard it before, and what they understand it to mean. (It is used to describe the imaginary harmonious sound of the planets in space.)

What do we learn about the space-bat-angel-dragon, and why he came to Earth? What made him cruel and greedy? How is the end of the story a fairy-tale ending?

## Structure

At the end of the story, ask the children to look back at the Contents page and consider the way the story is constructed in five chapters. Tell the children that the story is subtitled: 'A Children's Story in Five Nights'. Ask them to imagine they are reading it a chapter a night, and how each chapter leaves the story – with a mystery to be solved, or a happy 'ending'. What effect does this have on the story? Does it make you want to read on to find out what happens?

Finally, discuss the book more generally with the children. Did they enjoy reading it? Which part do they like best? Who is their favourite character? Is there any part they did not like? Encourage them to support their answers with reasons.

# Shared reading

## Extract 1

● Read an enlarged copy of the first extract.
● Ask the children to explain what has happened. How do they feel about it? Encourage them to support their responses (for example, pity, sadness, excitement) with reasons.
● Circle the word 'CRASSSHHH!' Ask the children how the writer adds to the impact of the word. (Altered, onomatapoeic spelling.)
● Underline examples of repetition (for example: 'He was in the pit. The Iron Man had fallen into the pit…' and, 'He ran, he ran…'). Ask the children what effect the repetition of words

has. (It speeds up the pace and conveys the boy's excitement.)
● Encourage the children to consider how the Iron Man might be feeling. What evidence is there that he has feelings? (Eyes changing colour, the sounds of cogs inside him screeching, the roaring as he is covered with earth.) What do they think each colour represents? Anger? Confusion?
● Ask the children how the farmers feel when they have trapped the Iron Man. (When the farmers saw…they sent up a great cheer.)

## Extract 2

● Read an enlarged copy of Extract 2.
● Ask the children how the Iron Man is feeling now. Why?
● Discuss why moving the Iron Man to the scrap-metal yard is a clever solution. How does it help the farmers as well as the Iron Man? (Their scrap metal is disposed of and not left in a tip.) Broaden the discussion to the environmental issue of waste. How has the Iron Man been transformed from being a threat and a problem to being a help?
● Ask the children to find words and phrases that describe scrap metal as if it is delicious food.

Circle the phrase 'crumbs of chrome' and revise alliteration.
● Discuss the similies which appear in the extract. ('…like a toffee', '…like a new gun barrell'.) How do these descriptions aid the reader's imagination?
● Invite the children to imagine a scrap-metal yard and try to think of different junk items and words or phrases that describe them as 'yummy' food.
● Underline the repetition of the verb 'ate' at the end of the extract. Ask the children to suggest why the writer repeats the same verb four times.

## Extract 3

● Read an enlarged copy of the third extract.
● Ask the children how the writer emphasises the huge size and scale of the dragon. Underline the metaphorical words 'this new sky'. What does it mean? (The sky created above Australia by the dragon's belly.) Let the children suggest adjectives to describe the size of the dragon. (Gargantuan, colossal, vast, massive.)
● Circle the adjective 'terrific', the adverb 'terribly' and the adjective 'terrible'. Can the children think of other words that share the same root? (Terror, terrify, terrorist.) Ask them to

count the repetitions of the adverb. What effect does this have?
● Underline the adjectives describing the dragon's features and ask the children to make nouns from them. Distinguish between adjectives ending in 'y' and past participles of verbs. (For example: scaly, knobbly, or clawed and fanged.)
● Focus on the questions at the end. Invite the children to rewrite them as statements and discuss how this changes the effect of the text. Which is most effective?

# Extract 1

CRASSSHHH!

The Iron Man vanished.

He was in the pit. The Iron Man had fallen into the pit. Hogarth went close. The earth was shaking as the Iron Man struggled underground. Hogarth peered over the torn edge of the great pit. Far below, two deep red headlamps glared up at him from the pitch blackness. He could hear the Iron Man's insides grinding down there and it sounded like a big lorry grinding its gears on a steep hill. Hogarth set off. He ran, he ran, home – home with the great news. And as he passed the cottages on the way, and as he turned down the lane towards his father's farm, he was shouting "The Iron Man's in the trap!" and "We've caught the Iron Giant."

When the farmers saw the Iron Man wallowing in their deep pit, they sent up a great cheer. He glared up towards them, his eyes burned from red to purple, from purple to white, from white to fiery whirling black and red, and the cogs inside him ground and screeched, but he could not climb out of the steep-sided pit.

Then under the lights of car headlamps, the farmers brought bulldozers and earth-pushers, and they began to push in on top of the struggling Iron Man all the earth they had dug when they first made the pit and that had been piled off to one side.

The Iron Man roared again as the earth began to fall on him. But soon he roared no more. Soon the pit was full of earth. Soon the Iron Man was buried silent, packed down under all the soil, while the farmers piled the earth over him in a mound and in a hill.

SCHOLASTIC
www.scholastic.co.uk

READ & RESPOND: Activities based on The Iron Man

# Extract 2

At last they came to the town, and there was a great scrap-metal yard. Everything was there, old cars by the hundred, old trucks, old railway engines, old stoves, old refrigerators, old springs, bedsteads, bicycles, girders, gates, pans – all the scrap iron of the region was piled up there, rusting away.

"There," cried Hogarth. "Eat all you can."

The Iron Man gazed, and his eyes turned red. He kneeled down in the yard, he stretched out on one elbow. He picked up a greasy black stove and chewed it like a toffee. There were delicious crumbs of chrome on it. He followed that with a double-decker bedstead and the brass knobs made his eyes crackle with joy. Never before had the Iron Man eaten such delicacies. As he lay there, a big truck turned into the yard and unloaded a pile of rusty chain. The Iron Man lifted a handful and let it dangle into his mouth – better than any spaghetti.

So there they left him. It was an Iron Man's heaven. The farmers went back to their farms. Hogarth visited the Iron Man every few days. Now the Iron Man's eyes were constantly a happy blue. He was no longer rusty. His body gleamed blue, like a new gun barrel. And he ate, ate, ate, ate – endlessly.

# Extract 3

The thing had actually landed – and it was a terrific dragon.

Terribly black, terribly scaly, terribly knobbly, terribly horned, terribly hairy, terribly clawed, terribly fanged, with vast indescribably terrible eyes, each one as big as Switzerland. There it sat, covering the whole of Australia, its tail trailing away over Tasmania into the sea, its foreclaws on the headlands of the Gulf of Carpentaria. Luckily, the mountains and hills propped its belly up clear of the valleys, and the Australians could still move about in the pitch darkness, under this new sky, this low queer covering, of scales. They crowded towards the light that came in along its sides. Of course, whoever had been on a mountain-top when the dragon landed had been squashed flat. Nothing could be done about them. And there the horror sat, glaring out over the countries of the world.

What had it come for? What was going to happen to the world now this monstrosity had arrived?

# Plot, character and setting

## Order, order

> **Objective:** To map out the main stages of the story.
> **What you need:** Copies of *The Iron Man*, photocopiable page 15, flipchart, individual whiteboards and pens, computers (optional).
> **Cross-curricular links:** PSHE; ICT.

### What to do
● Read together the closing paragraphs of *The Iron Man*. Ask the children what they feel about the ending. Is it satisfactory? In what way is it similar to a fairy tale? Suggest that, like all fairy tales, the plot of *The Iron Man* contains problems that have to be resolved, before everything can end 'happily ever after'.
● Next, ask which characters face problems that have to be solved. Write down the children's answers on the flipchart. Challenge the children to summarise the problem that each character has to resolve. Record these suggestions.

● In pairs, ask the children to refer to the story and make notes on how each problem is resolved. Afterwards, bring the class back together and discuss the sequence of problem and resolution within the plot.
● Hand out the photocopiable sheet and ask the children to fill it in, then cut out the boxes and paste them in the correct order following the plot of the story. This could also be adapted to become an ICT activity.
● Listen to some of the children's explanations.

> **Differentiation**
> **For older/more able children:** Ask the children to arrange the boxes from the photocopiable sheet into flow charts which show the connection between problem and resolution.
> **For younger/less able children:** Encourage the children to think of any other significant elements in the plot and to add them to the photocopiable sheet.

## Hogarth's home

> **Objective:** To understand how settings influence events and incidents in stories and how they affect characters' behaviour.
> **What you need:** Copies of *The Iron Man*, flipchart, writing materials, individual whiteboards and pens.
> **Cross-curricular links:** Geography, Unit 6, Investigating our local area.

### What to do
● Read together the opening of Chapter 2 from: 'One evening a farmer's son…' to: 'The Iron Man had come back.'
● Ask the children what they learn about the place where Hogarth lives from this reading. Can they describe the countryside where he is fishing and pick out its main features? (Near the sea; in a river valley; near sheer cliffs, woods and fields.) Write some of their suggestions on the flipchart.
● Let the children work in pairs to scan the

story for any other features about the place where Hogarth lives. (Prompt with questions such as: What sort of farms are there? Do they have animals or crops or both?) The children should write down their findings on their whiteboards.
● Bring the class back together and ask the children for more suggestions to add to the flipchart.
● As a shared writing activity, compile a short description of this countryside, including the main features described in the text.
● Discuss the setting in the context of the book. Is it an important feature?

> **Differentiation**
> **For older/more able children:** Ask the children to imagine they are Hogarth and write a first-person description of his home.
> **For younger/less able children:** Let the children draw a picture of Hogarth's home and the surrounding countryside.

# Plot, character and setting

## Timelines

> **Objective:** To explore chronology in narrative, by mapping how much time passes in the course of the story.
> **What you need:** Copies of *The Iron Man*, flipchart, photocopiable page 16, pens.
> **Cross-curricular links:** History.

### What to do

● Look together at the chapter headings on the contents page. Ask the children how much time they imagine passes during the course of the story.
● Talk about the pace of the story. Ask the children if they can suggest any events that happen *quickly* (when the Iron Man crashes over the cliff), and *slowly* (when a grassy hill forms over the Iron Man).
● Read together the passage, in chapter 2, in which the farmers wait for the Iron Man to fall into their trap, beginning: 'Next morning…' to: 'Grass began to grow…' How long do the children think the farmers are waiting, and which words suggest that time is passing?
● Can the children identify another passage where people are waiting for something to happen? (When the star gets closer.)
● Read together Chapter 4 from: 'One day there came strange news…' to: '…that filled the night.' How much time do the children think has passed here?
● Hand out the photocopiable sheet for the children to complete.

> **Differentiation**
> **For older/more able children:** Ask the children to write down the chapter headings and summarise the main events in each.
> **For younger/less able children:** Let the children choose one chapter to summarise.

## Iron strength

> **Objective:** To investigate how characters are presented.
> **What you need:** Copies of *The Iron Man*, flipchart and pen.
> **Cross-curricular links:** Science, Unit 2D, Grouping and changing materials.

### What to do

● Discuss with the children the Iron Man's character. Divide the flipchart into two columns and make lists together of all the things known and unknown about him.
● Ask the children how they feel about the Iron Man when he falls over the cliff, or into the farmers' trap. How do they feel when he is undergoing the trial with the space-bat-angel-dragon?
● Challenge them to suggest adjectives to describe the Iron Man's character. Encourage them to give reasons, using the text.
● Discuss the surreal nature of the scene in the first chapter when the parts of the Iron Man reassemble into his body. Does the Iron Man seem like a robot or a living being? Focus on the way he communicates, first with Hogarth and then with the space-bat-angel-dragon.
● Summarise on the flipchart all the ways in which the Iron Man communicates in the story. (His eyes changing colour, responding to metallic sounds, giving commands and challenges.) Can the children suggest adjectives or phrases to describe how his voice might sound?

> **Differentiation**
> **For older/more able children:** Let groups imagine answers to some of the things not known about the Iron Man.
> **For younger/less able children:** Encourage pairs to take turns to write down one word describing the Iron Man and find supporting evidence from the text.

# Plot, character and setting

## Just how big?

> **Objective:** To identify and discuss main and recurring characters, evaluate their behaviour and justify views.
> **What you need:** Copies of *The Iron Man*, individual whiteboards and pens, flipchart.
> **Cross-curricular links:** Design and technology, Unit 3C, Moving monsters.

### What to do

● Write on the flipchart: 'He really was a monster' and, 'The monster stared down [at the Iron Man]'. Ask the children whom they think the word 'monster' refers to in each case. Refer to chapters 3 and 5, where the sentences are used. What does the word 'monster' suggest to the children? Write answers on the flipchart.
● Divide the class into two groups, one to focus on the Iron Man, the other on the space-bat-angel-dragon. Ask each group to write down all the 'monsterish' things they can about their character, referring to the text. Then bring the class together, and record the children's suggestions on the flipchart.
● Discuss the idea that monsters in fairy tales can sometimes have a kind and caring side – like the beast in 'Beauty and the Beast', or in *Shrek*, the popular animation film. Are the Iron Man and the space-bat-angel-dragon really 'kind' monsters? Why? (The Iron Man is willing to sacrifice himself to protect the world; the space-bat-angel-dragon was led astray and is really a peaceful star spirit.)

> **Differentiation**
> **For older/more able children:** Ask groups to discuss how these two characters compare with other fairy-tale monsters.
> **For younger/less able children:** Encourage groups to discuss what makes a monster scary.

## Sizes and similes

> **Objective:** To refer to significant aspects of the text, and to know language is used to create them, for example, use of adjectives for description.
> **What you need:** Copies of *The Iron Man*, photocopiable page 17, writing materials, flipchart.
> **Cross-curricular links:** Mathematics.

### What to do

● Discuss together the theme of 'bigness' in the story. How is 'big' seen – as a good or bad thing? Elicit which big things are described in the story and how they are a threat, to the farmers, and later the people of the world. (The Iron Man, the growing star and the space-bat-angel-dragon.)
● Ask the children how the writer conveys the huge size of the Iron Man and the space-bat-angel-dragon. (By comparing them to familiar things.) What does the author compare them with? (Cattle truck, cranes, tall tree for the Iron Man, and whole countries for the space-bat-angel-dragon.) Remind the children that similes and comparison can help the reader form a picture of something unfamiliar.
● Hand out the photocopiable sheet and ask the children to fill it in.
● Afterwards, go through the answers as a class and write a list of things that are used to emphasise huge size on the flipchart:
  ● Iron Man: taller – *house*; head – *bedroom*; footprints – *single bed*; chest – *cattle truck*; arms – *crane*.
  ● Space-bat-angel-dragon: eyes – *Switzerland*; head – *Italy*; tongue – *Trans-Siberian railway*; stomach – *Germany*.

> **Differentiation**
> **For older/more able children:** Ask the children to think of their own similes to describe the Iron Man.
> **For younger/less able children:** Let the children draw a picture that illustrates the huge size of the Iron Man.

# Plot, character and setting

## Storyboard

> **Objective:** To retell main points of a story in sequence.
> **What you need:** Copies of *The Iron Man*, photocopiable page 18, writing materials, individual whiteboards and pens.
> **Cross-curricular links:** Art and design.

### What to do

● Read together at pace Chapter 2 from the beginning to: 'They were certain now that they'd get him.' Discuss the main events that happen in this sequence.

● Ask the children to imagine that they are going to direct a film of this part of the story. First of all, they have to map out the sequence of events. Tell them that, for a film or cartoon, this is often done on a storyboard, as a sequence of pictures.

● Hand out the photocopiable sheet. Explain to the children that they are going to use the boxes to write briefing notes for an illustrator who is going to draw a storyboard showing what happens. They should first work in pairs and use their whiteboards to make a list of the main scenes they want to include.

● Ask the children to fill in their storyboards individually, with the brief for each picture. They should give each scene a title, and include the setting, characters and notes about the action. For example, title: The Iron Man arrives; setting: the beach and cliffs, it is night-time; characters: The Iron Man, seagulls; Action: Iron Man steps forward and falls off the cliffs, the seagulls fly overhead.

● When they have finished the brief, they can go back into pairs and try drawing the storyboard pictures following their partner's brief.

> **Differentiation**
> **For older/more able children:** Ask the children to use their storyboards to map out another episode.
> **For younger/less able children:** Let the children complete their storyboard in pictures.

## In the news

> **Objective:** To distinguish between first and third person accounts.
> **What you need:** Copies of *The Iron Man*, writing materials.
> **Cross-curricular links:** Drama.

### What to do

● Read together Chapter 3, from the beginning to: 'They did not look back.'

● Divide the class into groups of five. In each group, four will play the role of the mother, father and children who are having the picnic. The fifth will play a newspaper reporter who interviews them after their ordeal.

● Tell the children that each group is going to prepare a short scene as if the family is being interviewed about their picnic scare for a television news bulletin.

● Explain that the family members need to imagine the picnic scene as if it happened to them – and retell it as a first-person account.

● When each group has decided on their roles, they should first discuss what they are going to say. They can refer back to the text and make notes on what each family member is going to describe. They should also list questions for the reporter to ask, including how they felt, and when and where the drama happened.

● When they have prepared a scene, ask the groups to perform it in front of the class.

> **Differentiation**
> **For older/more able children:** Encourage the children to use the interview material to write a newspaper report.
> **For younger/less able children:** Let the children work in pairs and perform one-to-one interviews.

# Plot, character and setting

# Order, order

Explain how each of the following is significant in the plot of *The Iron Man*. When you have finished, cut and paste the boxes in the order in which they feature in the story.

| A red star | Missing farm machinery | A missile and rocket attack |
|---|---|---|
| A trap | Music of the spheres | A test of strength |
| A scrapyard | | |

Illustration © Tom Gauld

# Timelines

Write down some events in the story that happen on a single day:

Write down some events that happen over a few days:

Write down some events in the story that happen over months or years:

Illustration © Tom Gauld

READ & RESPOND: Activities based on The Iron Man

# Sizes and similes

**Complete these similes describing the Iron Man:**

He is taller than _____

His head is as big as _____

His footprints are the size of _____

His chest is as big as _____

His arms are like _____

**Complete these similes describing the space-bat-angel-dragon:**

His eyes are as big as _____

His head is the size of _____

His tongue is longer than _____

His stomach is the size of _____

Illustration © Tom Gauld

SECTION
4

# Storyboard

Write notes explaining what each scene in the storyboard should show. Include instructions for characters, setting and action. Add more boxes on the other side of the sheet if you need to.

**Scene 1**

Title _____

Setting _____

Characters _____

_____

Action _____

_____

_____

**Scene 2**

Title _____

Setting _____

Characters _____

_____

Action _____

_____

_____

**Scene 3**

Title _____

Setting _____

Characters _____

_____

Action _____

_____

_____

**Scene 4**

Title _____

Setting _____

Characters _____

_____

Action _____

_____

_____

**Scene 5**

Title _____

Setting _____

Characters _____

_____

Action _____

_____

_____

**Scene 6**

Title _____

Setting _____

Characters _____

_____

Action _____

_____

_____

www.scholastic.co.uk

# Talk about it

## Good beginnings

> **Objective:** To analyse the features of a good opening and compare a number of story openings.
> **What you need:** Copies of *The Iron Man* and *The Iron Woman*, individual whiteboards and pens, photocopiable page 22.

### What to do
● Tell the children that after he wrote *The Iron Man*, Ted Hughes wrote a sequel called *The Iron Woman*. They are going to compare the openings of these two stories.
● Read from the start of *The Iron Woman* to: 'It must be an earthquake!' Can the children suggest what the earthquake might be? What does Lucy observe that makes her feel something is wrong?
● Now re-read together the beginning of *The Iron Man* to: '…silent and unmoving.'
● Ask the children which story opening they prefer, giving reasons. Do the two openings have anything in common? What is the atmosphere in each?
● Suggest that both openings ask lots of unanswered questions. Explain that this is one of the ways the author builds suspense.
● Hand out the photocopiable sheet to each child. Ask the children to work in pairs: one child should consider the first scene from *The Iron Man*, and the other *The Iron Woman*.
● Ask the children to complete the part that relates to their book. Then, each pair should discuss their findings and work together to complete the rest of their sheet.
● Ask pairs to join up to discuss their answers.

> **Differentiation**
> **For older/more able children:** Ask groups to consider answers to the unanswered questions on the photocopiable sheet.
> **For younger/less able children:** Let groups focus on the unanswered questions in *The Iron Man*.

## The plan

> **Objective:** To discuss characters' feelings; behaviour, for example, fair, unreasonable, brave or foolish.
> **What you need:** Copies of *The Iron Man*, flipchart, individual whiteboards and pens.
> **Cross-curricular links:** PSHE.

### What to do
● Read together the section in Chapter 2 beginning: 'Next morning all the farmers were shouting with anger…' to: 'They were certain now that they'd get him.'
● Discuss with the children how the farmers are feeling. Write suggested words and phrases on the flipchart.
● Ask the children how the farmers see the Iron Man. What adjectives might they use to describe him? What might the farmers write on a 'wanted' poster? Write suggestions on the flipchart.
● What are the farmers frightened the Iron Man may start to do? (Eat things other than iron.) Why do they feel they cannot call in the police or the army? (They would not be believed.)
● Divide the children into two groups, challenging them to prepare a short drama. The first group should prepare a scene in which the farmers discuss the Iron Man and decide to do something to stop him. The second should prepare a scene in which the farmers think up and put into action their plan.
● Ask each group to perform its scene. Talk to each group and discuss why they chose to portray the scene in that particular way.

> **Differentiation**
> **For older/more able children:** Let the children work in pairs, one child defending the Iron Man, the other accusing him.
> **For younger/less able children:** Ask the children to discuss different ways of dealing with the Iron Man.

# Talk about it

## Persuasion

> **Objective:** To retell the main points of the story in sequence.
> **What you need:** Copies of *The Iron Man*, flipchart, individual whiteboards and pens, photocopiable page 23.
> **Cross-curricular links:** Geography, Unit 8, Improving the environment; Citizenship.

### What to do

● Challenge the children to find three episodes in the book where Hogarth has to use his persuasive powers to convince others.
● Divide the flipchart into two columns. Ask the children to identify in each episode the person or people Hogarth is trying to persuade and to what purpose.
● Read aloud the paragraph in Chapter 3 from: 'When the farmers realized that the Iron Man had freed himself...' to: 'Yes, they would give Hogarth's idea a trial.'
● Ask the children, in pairs, to discuss what the farmers wanted to do. (Call the army.) What do they think Hogarth might have said to convince them otherwise? They should write down their ideas on their whiteboards.
● Bring the class together to discuss their ideas. Do the children think Hogarth's plan worked? How does it help the people of the world later?
● Hand out the photocopiable sheet and ask the children to fill them in, discussing their findings in pairs.

> **Differentiation**
> **For older/more able children:** Ask groups of four to role-play a scene in which Hogarth has to convince his family he has seen an iron giant.
> **For younger/less able children:** Let pairs role-play a scene in which the Iron Man has eaten their parents' car and they have to defend him.

## Hybrids

> **Objective:** To identify and classify the features of myths, for example, fantastical beasts in legend.
> **What you need:** Flipchart and pen, picture references to mythical hybrid beasts (centaurs, minotaurs and griffins).
> **Cross-curricular links:** Design and technology, Unit 3C, Moving monsters.

### What to do

● Challenge the children to describe the space monster. Can they remember any words used in the text? Write them down on the flipchart.
● Ask the children why they think the writer has used a hybrid name with four parts: space-bat-angel-dragon? (It has features of all of them.) Take the words in turn and ask the children what each suggests in terms of the look or behaviour of the monster. What does the juxtaposition of angel-dragon suggest? (Something wonderful and terrifying at once.)
● Discuss the nature of the monster, good or bad. What does it do or say that makes it seem bad? (It wants to be fed.) What happens to change this perception? (The Iron Man challenges him and he loses, apologises and explains what happened.)
● Talk about hybrid monsters from myths. Display your pictures and ask the children to describe what they look like. Which look most frightening? Why?
● Challenge the children to suggest creatures that could be combined to create new frightening monsters. As a class, collate names for these hybrid creatures.

> **Differentiation**
> **For older/more able children:** Ask pairs to invent a hybrid creature, creating a compound name for it and writing a short description.
> **For younger/less able children:** Let small groups invent a hybrid creature, thinking of ways to describe it.

# Talk about it

## Hidden messages

> **Objective:** To identify typical story themes, for example, trial and forfeits, good over evil, weak over strong, wise over foolish.
> **What you need:** Copies of *The Iron Man*.
> **Cross-curricular links:** RE.

### What to do

● Read Chapter 4 beginning: 'For a whole day…' to: 'Human weapons had no effect on it.'
● Discuss together why the people of the world felt they had to act, and what they did. (Attacked the space-bat-angel-dragon.) Was it a good plan? Why not?
● Challenge the children to recall how the farmers tried to get rid of the Iron Man. (They laid a trap.) What were they going to do if Hogarth's plan failed? (Call in the army.)
● Elicit from the children the message of the story. (War is not the way to solve problems.)
● Talk about what people and countries go to war over. (Ownership of land or difference of religion.) Is war ever the only option or are there always alternatives? (Be sensitive to individual children's circumstances.)
● Read the end of the story (from: '"Haven't you heard of the music of the spheres?" asked the dragon.'). How did people change when the space-bat-angel-dragon started singing? Remind the children of the 'angel' part of the dragon's name. Suggest that there are echoes of the Christian theme of angels singing of peace. How might things be different if Hogarth had not intervened? (The space-bat-angel-dragon may have acted upon his threat and licked civilisation off the planet.)

> **Differentiation**
> **For older/more able children:** Encourage groups to identify other themes in the book.
> **For younger/less able children:** Ask groups to discuss what they think about the ending.

## Reality or fantasy?

> **Objective:** To understand how writers create imaginary worlds.
> **What you need:** Copies of *The Iron Man*, photocopiable page 24, writing materials.

### What to do

● Look together at the cover illustration of *The Iron Man*. What sort of story is suggested by the illustration and the title: realistic or imaginary?
● Ask the children what sort of world they think the Iron Man comes from. Can they imagine where he lived before the story begins?
● Can they remember where the space-bat-angel-dragon comes from, and how it describes itself? (A star spirit that flies in space or makes music.) What sort of story do dragons usually appear in? (Fairy tales and fantasy stories.)
● What genre do the children think *The Iron Man* belongs to – science fiction, realistic stories, myth, fable or fairy story? Encourage them to give reasons.
● Hand out photocopiable page 24. Divide the class into two groups.
● Challenge one group to search for all the realistic elements relating to character, setting and plot (farming, picnics, astronomers), and the other to search for fantasy elements (the Iron Man, the space-bat-angel-dragon, trial by fire). Ask both groups to record their answers on the photocopiable sheet.
● Bring the class back together to discuss their findings. Let the children complete the other half of the sheet.

> **Differentiation**
> **For older/more able children:** Ask the children to discuss the mood created in the illustrations.
> **For younger/less able children:** Encourage the children to explain which illustration they like best.

# Good beginnings

|  | *The Iron Man* | *The Iron Woman* |
|---|---|---|
| Which character(s) appear(s) in the opening scene? |  |  |
| Explain briefly what happens. |  |  |
| What do we find out in this scene? |  |  |
| What questions are left unanswered? |  |  |
| What are the main differences and similarities between the Iron Man and the Iron Woman? |  |  |

# Persuasion

What do you think Hogarth says to his father to persuade him he has seen an iron man?

What do you think Hogarth says to the farmers to persuade them to try his plan?

Illustration © Tom Gauld

What might Hogarth say about their plan?

What do you think Hogarth says to the Iron Man to persuade him to challenge the space-bat-angel-dragon?

What reasons could Hogarth give to persuade the Iron Man?

# Reality or fantasy?

Write examples of each from *The Iron Man*.

| **Realistic** |
|---|
| Characters _____ |
| _____ |
| _____ |
| Setting _____ |
| _____ |
| _____ |
| _____ |
| Plot _____ |
| _____ |
| _____ |
| _____ |
| _____ |
| _____ |
| _____ |

Illustration © Tom Gauld

| **Fantastical** |
|---|
| Characters _____ |
| _____ |
| Setting _____ |
| _____ |
| Plot _____ |
| _____ |
| _____ |

# Get writing

## A good read

> **Objective:** To map out texts showing development and structure, for example, its high and low points.
> **What you need:** Copies of *The Iron Man*, individual whiteboards and pens, flipchart, books with good back-cover blurbs.
> **Cross-curricular links:** Science, Unit 3C, Characteristics of materials; Unit 6D, Reversible and irreversible changes (section 4).

### What to do
● Ask the children which events in *The Iron Man* they find most memorable. Encourage them to give reasons.
● Challenge the children to remember the main sequence of events in the story. Look at the contents page and ask the children to recall what happens in each chapter.
● Arrange the children in groups of three. Ask each to make a list of events on their whiteboards, one child concentrating on the Iron Man, the second on the space-bat-angel-dragon and the third on Hogarth. Then bring the class back together and collate their suggestions.
● Ask the children to identify how and when the writer uses suspense. Which are the key episodes for building suspense? (The farmers waiting to trap the Iron Man; the picnic scene; the star growing.)
● Show the class your selection of books with back-cover blurbs. Ask the children to use the ideas on the flipchart to write a blurb for *The Iron Man*.

> **Differentiation**
> **For older/more able children:** Ask pairs to invent quotes for the book blurbs.
> **For younger/less able children:** In pairs, ask the children to write a paragraph on which bit of the story they find most exciting.

## Barrrump!

> **Objective:** To write own examples of descriptive, expressive language based on those read.
> **What you need:** Copies of *The Iron Man*, writing materials, photocopiable page 28, flipchart and pen, map of the world.
> **Cross-curricular links:** Geography.

### What to do
● Read Chapter 4 together, from: 'What was coming out of the giant star?' to: '…glaring out over the countries of the world.'
● Focus on the sentences that describe the space-bat-angel-dragon's landing on Australia. Discuss the onomatopoeic word 'Barrrump!' What does it convey?
● Invite the children to read out the effects of the landing. List words on the flipchart. Remind the children that the dragon lands heavily twice more – during the test of strength. Challenge them to find the relevant paragraphs and add any other words to your list.
● Ask the children how the writer conveys the vast size of the dragon. Display your world map and ask a volunteer to indicate the area that the dragon covers. Compare it with the United Kingdom.
● Encourage the children to imagine how the dragon lying on Australia might interfere with people's lives, for example, ships encountering the tail at sea.
● Hand out the photocopiable sheet and challenge the children to imagine how the dragon's landing might impact on their own surroundings.

> **Differentiation**
> **For older/more able children:** Ask the children to write a description of living under the 'new sky'.
> **For younger/less able children:** Let the children write a list of what they learn about the dragon as it lands on Australia.

# Get writing

## Playtime

> **Objective:** To prepare a short section of a story as a script, for example, using stage directions, location/ setting.
> **What you need:** Copies of *The Iron Man*, writing materials, flipchart, playscript showing stage directions (optional).
> **Cross-curricular links:** Drama.

### What to do

● Read together the beginning of Chapter 2, as far as: '…as fast as he could, homeward.'
● Ask the children to identify all the characters who feature in this episode. Make a list on the flipchart.
● Let the children suggest words for how each character reacts when they see or hear about the Iron Man. What emotions are they feeling? Write down their suggestions.
● Encourage the children to look closely at the paragraphs from: 'So he got home at last…' to the end of the section. Can they identify any words of direct speech? (For example: His feet will have left tracks in the earth.) Can they suggest where they could put in speech marks to make it clear which words are direct speech?
● Ask the children if they can write any other words of direct speech to replace reported speech in the episode. What might the farmers say to each other when they find the broken tractor? For example: 'Where's my tractor?' said Fred.
● Challenge the children to write a playscript relating the episode. They should include speech and stage directions. (Refer to your sample playscript if appropriate.)

> **Differentiation**
> **For older/more able children:** Ask the children to write a short playscript of another episode.
> **For younger/less able children:** Encourage the children to write character notes (on age, looks, dress) for their playscript.

## In my view

> **Objective:** To write a first-person account.
> **What you need:** Copies of *The Iron Man*, writing materials, flipchart, individual whiteboards and pens.
> **Cross-curricular links:** Geography, Unit 23, Investigating coasts.

### What to do

● Read together the episode in Chapter 1 from: 'Just before dawn…' to: '…as the sun rose over the sea and the day came.'
● Discuss with the children what is happening here. Ask them what role the seagulls play. (They are the only observers.) They also play a role in reconstructing the Iron Man. Can the children explain how? (They bring one of the eyes and hands together.)
● Ask the children to work out the chronological sequence in which the body parts find each other and reassemble. They should start with 'first eye' and 'first hand' and so on. Write the body parts in list order on the flipchart.
● Encourage the children to imagine that they are beachcombers, taking a walk in the early morning. First, they see the seagull find the eye; then they witness the scene as the Iron Man reassembles himself.
● Challenge them to write a description of the experience in the first person, as if they are writing a diary entry. Encourage them to express how they feel.
● Share these descriptions as a class.

> **Differentiation**
> **For older/more able children:** Ask the children to write an alternative first-person account as the Iron Man.
> **For younger/less able children:** Let the children write a short recount of how the Iron Man puts himself back together.

# Get writing

## Headlines

> **Objective:** To plot a sequence of episodes modelled on a known story as a plan for writing.
> **What you need:** Copies of *The Iron Man*, photocopiable page 29, writing materials, flipchart, computers (optional).
> **Cross-curricular links:** ICT; Art and design.

### What to do

● Read the beginning of Chapter 4 to: 'It was definitely coming straight at the earth.'
● Discuss together what is happening here. How would they feel if astronomers reported strange events like this suddenly happening in the sky?
● Encourage the children to consider how they would approach the story if they were a journalist – interviewing experts (astronomers) and eyewitnesses, and attempting to record the sequence of events as they happened.
● Ask the children to summarise the main sequence of events in chronological order. Write a bulleted list on the flipchart.
● Challenge the children to think of some snappy headlines that could be used for the front page of a newspaper reporting the story.
● Hand out the photocopiable sheet and explain that you want the children to to use this to plan their newspaper report. Remind them that they will need to record the sequence of events in chronological order. They can invent some quotes from expert astronomers and from frightened eyewitnesses to make their reports more interesting.

> **Differentiation**
> **For older/more able children:** Challenge the children to write up their report, perhaps using computers.
> **For younger/less able children:** Ask the children to draw a picture of astronomers and to include speech bubbles.

## Book review

> **Objectives:** To write a brief helpful review tailored for real audiences; to write a brief synopsis of a text, for example, for back-cover blurb.
> **What you need:** Copies of *The Iron Man*, photocopiable page 30, writing materials.

### What to do

● Explain to the children that they are going to plan a review of *The Iron Man*, incorporating information about the characters, events and hidden messages in the story as well as practical information on the author, illustrator and intended audience of the book.
● Divide the class into (four or five) small groups. Encourage the children to discuss their favourite parts of the story, and any parts they do not like.
● Ask them to talk in their groups about the messages that the story contains: that blindly waging war achieves nothing, while dialogue and other, more peaceful methods may bring about reconciliation.
● Look together at the cover and illustrations in the book. How would the children describe the style of the artist? How do they capture the mood of the story? What concepts or ideas from the story do they help to convey? (The huge scale of the iron giant, the loneliness of Hogarth, a bleak, rather hostile setting.)
● Hand out the photocopiable sheet and ask the children to use their ideas to fill it in, as a planning sheet for a book review.
● Ask the children to discuss their ideas and explain the reasons behind their choices in pairs or small groups.

> **Differentiation**
> **For older/more able children:** Ask the children to write up their book review.
> **For younger/less able children:** Let the children complete the photocopiable sheet in pairs.

# Get writing

# Barrrump!

Write down some onomatopoeic words to describe the dragon landing – you can make them up!

Where does the dragon land? List the countries, seas and oceans it covers.

What else happens around the world each time it lands?

Write down some things that might happen around you if it happened… when you were at home:

when you were at school:

Illustration © Tom Gauld

# $G$et writing

# Headlines

Write a snappy headline for your news report.

Explain what has been happening in the skies, listing the key points.

Invent a quote from an expert astronomer, giving his or her theory on what is happening – and remember to include their name!

Write quotes from two or more worried onlookers saying how they feel about these strange events.

# Get writing

# Book review

*The Iron Man*

Author:

Illustrator:

Illustration © Tom Gauld

Choose your favourite part of the story and explain why you like it:

Write about any parts you do not like and explain why:

Describe how the illustrations help convey the mood and ideas of the story:

Who would you recommend this book to and why?

# Assessment

## Assessment advice

Assessment is an ongoing process, enabling teachers and children to consolidate learning, and set new targets as the children progress. Practical written work and classroom discussion can both be used to indicate a child's level of progress, and highlight areas of strength as well as those skills that need further development.

In *Read & Respond*, the children will be asked to complete a range of activities to develop their speaking, listening, reading and writing skills.

These skill areas can all be assessed using written work and classroom observations of individual, paired and group work. As many of the activities will be reinforcing understanding, earlier work can often be used as a useful reference to remind them of what they have learned, and to consolidate that learning.

The assessment activity on photocopiable page 32 could be used as part of a record of children's progress.

## Story and fairy-tale elements

> **Objective:** To write summaries of books or parts of books, deciding priorities relevant to purpose.
> **What you need:** Photocopiable page 32, flipchart, writing materials, the film *The Iron Giant*, copies of *The Iron Woman*.

### What to do

● Discuss together the main events and themes within *The Iron Man*. Ask the children to give their subjective opinions of the story, and to support their views with reasons. Ask them if it has encouraged them to read other work by Ted Hughes and, if so, why? Ensure all the children take part in the discussion. You will be able to make some judgements based on their verbal responses.

● If possible, watch the film version of the story *The Iron Giant*. Discuss with the children how close it is to the original story and how successful or not they think it is as an adaptation. What do they like or dislike about the treatment? If there is time, the class could go on to read Ted Hughes' sequel, *The Iron Woman*, and compare and contrast its themes, events and characters with *The Iron Man*.

● Discuss plot, setting and character as key ingredients in this, and any other story. Ask the children which of these key aspects they would think about first when planning a story and why.

● Write on the flipchart the cover blurb from the *Observer*, describing the story: 'Reckoned one of the greatest of modern fairy tales.' Ask the children to come up with the titles of some familiar fairy tales. Can the children suggest features they would expect in stories of this kind? (Magical events and settings, heroes and heroines, happy endings and so on.) Ask the children how *The Iron Man* falls into the genre of fairy tale. What similarities are there? Can they say what makes it 'modern' compared to traditional fairy stories?

● Ask the children to work on their own to complete the photocopiable sheet, using their knowledge of *The Iron Man*. Encourage them to refer back to the story as closely as possible with examples.

# Story and fairy-tale elements

**Story elements**

What is the title of the story? _____

Who are the main characters? _____

What are the main events? _____

_____

What are the main themes? _____

_____

**Fairy-tale elements**

What happens more than once in the story? _____

_____

What test or trial takes place?

_____

_____

_____

How is it a 'fairy-tale' ending?

_____

_____

_____

Illustration © Tom Gauld